I0811657

HOW TO DRAW BOOK OF MORMON CHARACTERS

ISBN 13: 978-1-4621-2343-8

Published by CFI, an imprint of Cedar Fort, Inc.
2373 W. 700 S., Springville, UT 84663
Distributed by Cedar Fort, Inc., www.cedarfort.com

Library of Congress Control Number: 2018960293

Cover and page design by Jeff Harvey
Cover design © 2019 Cedar Fort, Inc.
Edited by Kaitlin Barwick

Printed in the United States of America

10 9 8 7 6 5 4 3 2 1

Printed on acid-free paper

HOW TO DRAW BOOK OF MORMON CHARACTERS

JEFF HARVEY

CFI
An imprint of Cedar Fort, Inc.
Springville, Utah

AS YOU GO THROUGH THIS BOOK, MY HOPE IS THAT YOU WILL LEARN SOME DRAWING PRINCIPLES THAT YOU CAN USE IN ANY DRAWING. TO START OFF, I WILL HIGHLIGHT A FEW OF THE PRINCIPLES AND TECHINIQUES THAT WILL COME UP THROUGHOUT THE BOOK. YOU CAN USE THIS AS A GUIDE THAT YOU CAN REFER BACK TO AS YOU GO THROUGH THE BOOK OR EVEN WHEN YOU ARE DRAWING ON YOUR OWN.

SHAPES

IN STEP 1 OF EACH DRAWING, I LIKE TO BREAK THINGS DOWN INTO BASIC SHAPES. THESE CAN BE GREAT BUILDING BLOCKS TO START YOUR DRAWINGS. I ALSO LOVE SHAPES BECAUSE EACH ONE MEANS SOMETHING DIFFERENT.

CIRCLE—IT HELPS TO THINK OF THINGS THAT ARE ROUND: BALLS BOUNCE AND ROLL AROUND. THEY'RE UNSTABLE, BUT FUN. USING CIRCLES USUALLY MEANS GOOFY, MAYBE A BIT UNPREDICTABLE, BUT FUN OVERALL.

SQUARE—WHEN I THINK OF SQUARES (OR RECTANGLES) I THINK OFFICE BUILDINGS, DOORS, CABINETS—THINGS ARE GENERALLY BORING, BUT THEY **WORK**. CHARACTERS THAT ARE SQUARISH AREN'T VERY EXCITING, BUT THEY ARE USUALLY STRONG AND STEADY.

TRIANGLE—THIS ONE CAN BE A BIT TRICKY BECAUSE TRIANGLES ARE THE STRONGEST SHAPE, SO A TRIANGLE POSE SHOWS STRENGTH. BUT A GOOD RULE TO FOLLOW IF YOU USE AN ACTUAL SHARP TRIANGLE IS THAT IT REPRESENTS DANGER (THE MORE YOU USE, THE MORE DANGEROUS IT IS).

FOLDS

WITH EACH CHARACTER, THERE WILL BE LOTS OF DIFFERENT CLOTHING, BELTS, AND SASHES, BUT YOU STILL NEED TO SHOW THE FORMS UNDERNEATH. THE WAY TO DO THIS IS TO KNOW HOW CLOTHES FOLD AND SIT ON THE BODY. UNDERSTANDING THIS WILL HELP YOU KNOW WHAT FOLDS APPEAR WHEN YOUR CHARACTER BENDS AN ARM OR WEARS A BELT.

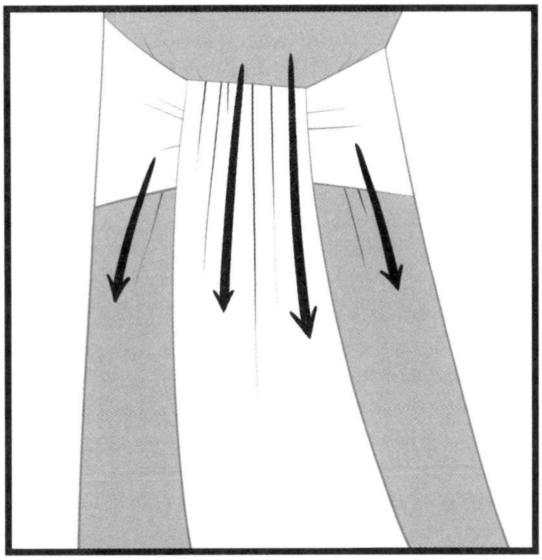

PIPE FOLD—THESE HAPPEN WHEN CLOTHING IS TIGHT OR BUNCHED UP AT ONE POINT AND HANGS DOWN LOOSELY.

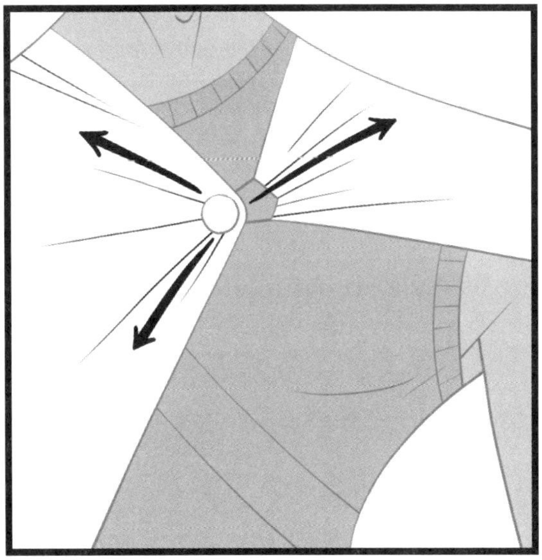

TENSION FOLD—THIS IS IN THE SAME FAMILY AS THE PIPE FOLD EXCEPT THEY ARE PULLED TIGHTLY AT TWO POINTS SO THEY DON'T NECESSARILY HANG STRAIGHT DOWN.

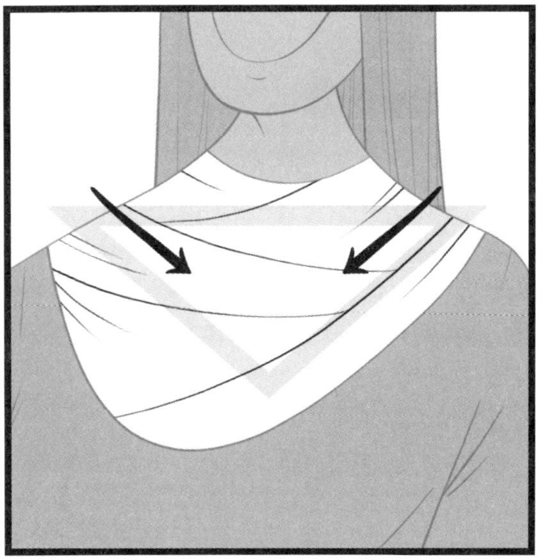

DIAPER FOLD—THIS HAPPENS WHEN A CLOTH IS HELD UP AT TWO POINTS AND HANGS DOWN IN THE MIDDLE, FORMING A TRIANGULAR SHAPE.

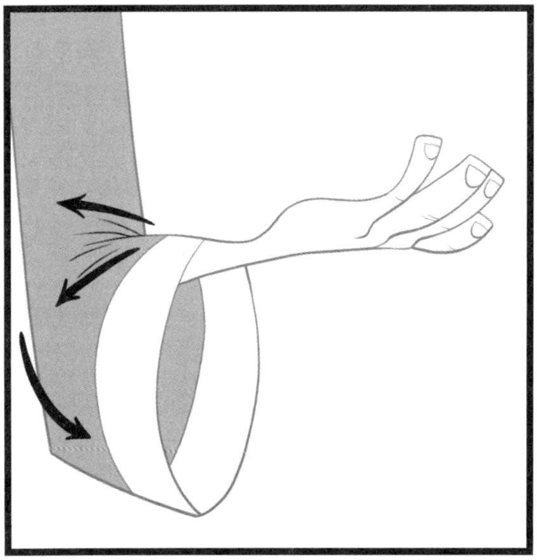

HALF-LOCK FOLD—THIS FOLD APPEARS WHEN JOINTS LIKE KNEES AND ELBOWS BEND. ONE SIDE BUNCHES UP WHILE THE OPPOSITE SIDE HANGS LOOSELY.

THERE ARE OTHER TYPES OF FOLDS YOU WILL SEE FROM DAY TO DAY, BUT SINCE WE ARE SIMPLIFYING THINGS IN THESE DRAWINGS, WE'LL STICK TO THESE.

TIPS & TECHNIQUES

FORESHORTENING IS USED TO SHOW WHEN SOMETHING IS EITHER COMING TOWARD OR MOVING AWAY FROM THE VIEWER. IN THIS CASE, WE WILL LOOK AT FORESHORTENING WITH AN ARM. THIS WILL BE HELPFUL AS YOU WORK THROUGH THE BOOK. REMEMBER, THIS APPLIES TO ANYTHING, NOT JUST ARMS.

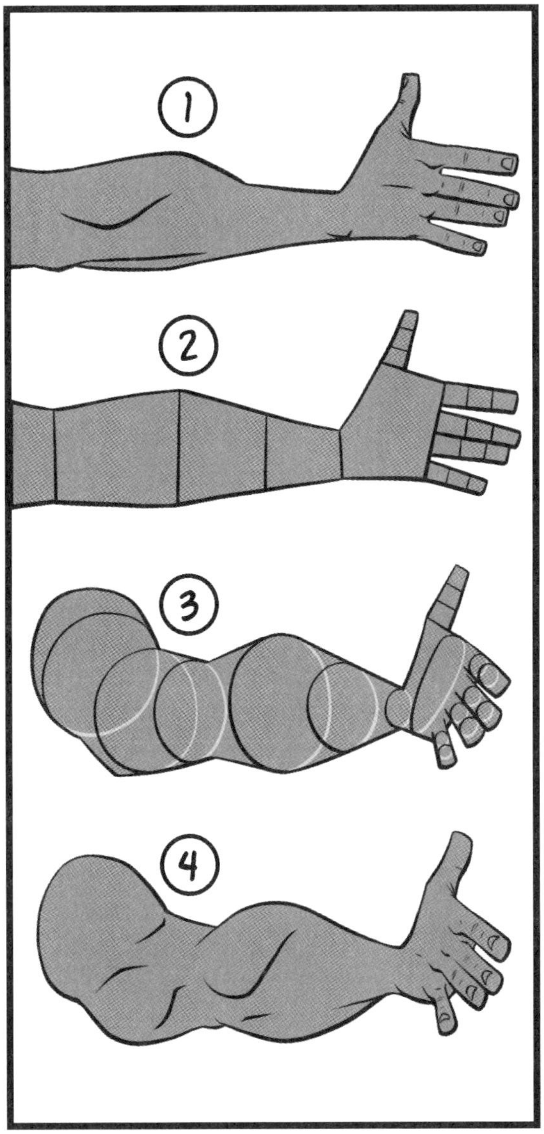

1—I'VE STARTED WITH A SIMPLE SIDE VIEW OF THE ARM. THIS EXAMPLE IS MORE DETAILED THAN THE DRAWINGS THROUGHOUT THE BOOK JUST TO SHOW IT APPLIES NO MATTER THE STYLE.

2—IMAGINE THAT THE ARM AND FINGERS ARE TUBES WITH CIRCLES DRAWN AROUND THE OUTSIDE.

3—TURN THE "TUBE." WHEN YOU DO THAT, THE CIRCLES TURN AS WELL, CAUSING THEM TO LOOK LIKE OVALS. THE MORE THEY TURN, THE WIDER THE OVALS BECOME.

4—USE THE NEW TUBE DRAWING TO DRAW IN THE FORM AND DETAILS.

"STRAIGHTS AND CURVES," OR ***"STRAIGHTS AGAINST CURVES,"*** IS A TERM ARTISTS USE A LOT. THIS MEANS IN EVERY DRAWING YOU SHOULD BALANCE THE AMOUNT OF STRAIGHT AND CURVED LINES YOU USE; PARTICULARLY YOU SHOULD USE THEM OPPOSITE OF EACH OTHER. LET'S LOOK AT THE ARM FROM THE PREVIOUS EXAMPLE:

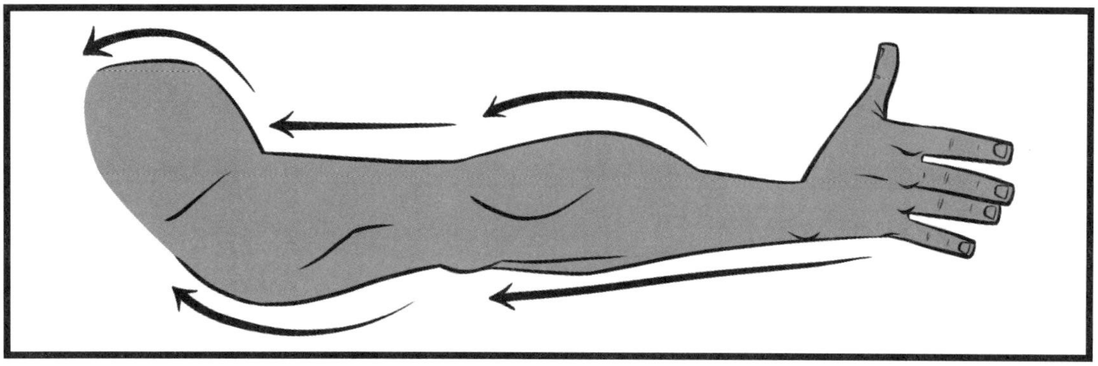

NOT ONLY ARE THE STRAIGHTS AND CURVES OPPOSITE FROM EACH OTHER, BUT EACH SIDE ALSO REPEATS CURVE, STRAIGHT, CURVE. THIS MIGHT NOT ALWAYS BE THE CASE, BUT YOU SHOULD TRY TO FIND A NICE BALANCE SIMILAR TO THIS. NOW LET'S LOOK AT WHEN YOU USE ONLY STRAIGHTS OR CURVES:

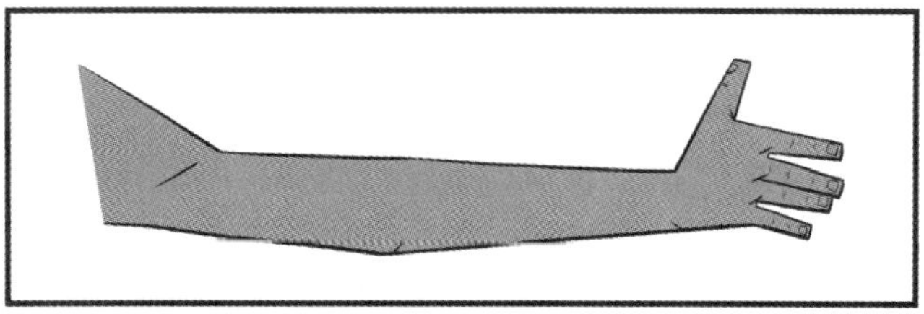

WHEN ONLY STRAIGHT LINES ARE USED, THE ARM LOOKS LIFELESS AND NOT REAL.

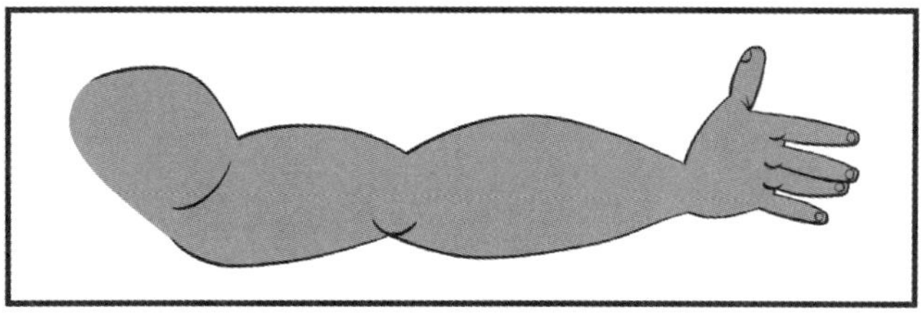

WHEN ONLY CURVES ARE USED, THE ARM LOOKS MORE LIKE A BALLOON ANIMAL.

WHILE YOU DON'T NECESSARILY HAVE TO WORRY ABOUT EVERY SINGLE LINE AND MAKING SURE IT FOLLOWS THIS PRINCIPLE, BE SURE TO AVOID USING ONLY STRAIGHTS OR ONLY CURVES SO THAT YOUR DRAWING DOESN'T LOOK LIKE THE ARMS ABOVE.

TO GO ALONG WITH THE STRAIGHTS AGAINST CURVES PRINCIPLE, WHENEVER YOU DRAW PEOPLE, A GOOD RULE TO KEEP IN MIND IS TO USE ***CONVEX*** LINES ALONG THE OUTSIDE, NOT ***CONCAVE***. CONVEX MEANS THAT THE LINE CURVES OUT WHILE CONCAVE LINES CURVE IN. IF YOU LOOK AT THE ARM IN THE PREVIOUS EXAMPLE, ALL OF THE CURVES GO OUT FROM THE FORM, AND THE ONLY OTHER LINES ARE STRAIGHT. ONCE THE LINES START CURVING IN, IT BEGINS TO LOOK FUNNY AND NOT HUMAN.

FINALLY, IN THE LAST STEP OF EACH CHARACTER, I ALWAYS RECOMMEND THAT YOU EITHER COLOR OR DARKEN AREAS IN YOUR DRAWING. DOING THIS ALLOWS YOU TO USE ***CONTRAST*** TO DRAW ATTENTION TO WHATEVER YOU WANT. LOOK AT THE TWO RECTANGLES BELOW:

IF YOU WERE TO CONTINUE LOOKING AT THESE, YOUR EYES WOULD KEEP COMING BACK TO THE RECTANGLE ON THE LEFT. THAT'S BECAUSE OF CONTRAST. THAT MEANS THERE IS AN AREA OF TWO VERY DIFFERENT THINGS, IN THIS CASE BLACK AND WHITE. WHEN THEY ARE RIGHT NEXT TO EACH OTHER, IT CREATES INTEREST AND DRAWS YOUR EYE THERE. MAKE SURE TO USE CONTRAST TO DRAW THE EYE WHEREVER YOU WANT IT.

YOU CAN ALSO CREATE AREAS OF INTEREST BY ***BREAKING UP THE SHAPE.*** JUST LIKE THE PREVIOUS EXAMPLE, STARTING OFF WITH JUST A BASIC SHAPE, WHILE SOMETIMES CAN BE WHAT YOU NEED, CAN ALSO BE BORING. TAKE A LOOK AT THIS EXAMPLE:

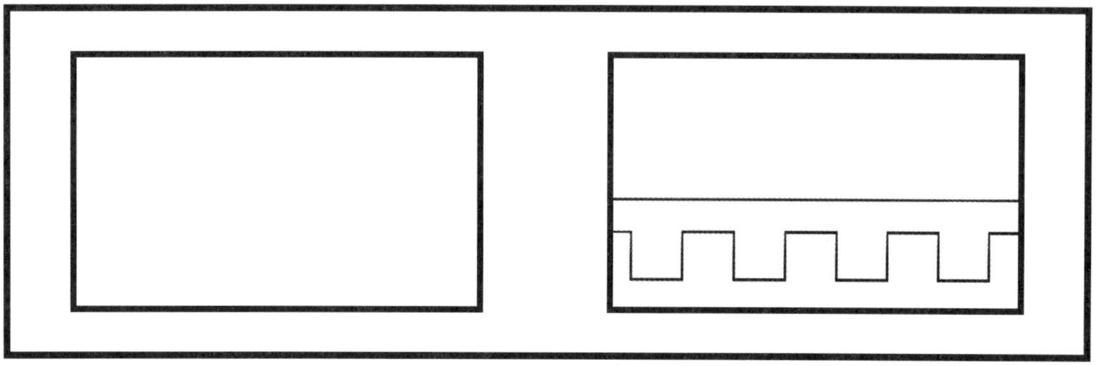

THE RECTANGLE ON THE RIGHT IS OBVIOUSLY MORE INTERESTING TO LOOK AT; IT AGAIN DRAWS THE EYE IN WITH ITS PATTERN. USING THIS, REMEMBER TO USE DECORATION ON CLOTHING WITH A PURPOSE. MAKE SURE YOU ARE PUTTING AREAS OF INTEREST WHERE YOU WANT YOUR AUDIENCE TO LOOK. THIS COMBINED WITH CONTRAST CAN BE A VERY POWERFUL TOOL. MAKE SURE YOU ARE CAREFUL—OVERUSING THESE CAN BE A BAD THING.

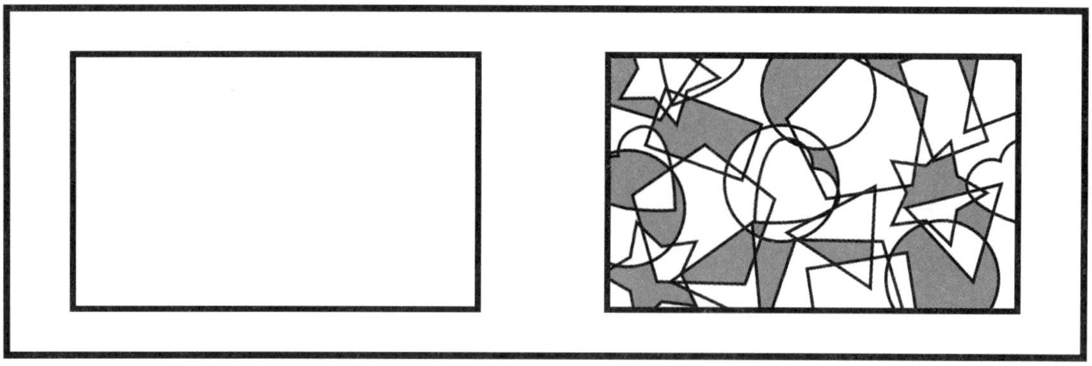

WHEN YOU LOOK AT THE TWO RECTANGLES ABOVE, ALTHOUGH THE RIGHT MAY BE INTERESTING, IT'S FAR TOO BUSY TO SEE WHAT IS HAPPENING AND MAY MAKE THE FIRST RECTANGLE THE RIGHT CHOICE. THERE IS NO RULE THAT STATES WHEN YOU SHOULD AND SHOULDN'T USE THESE PRINCIPLES. JUST MAKE SURE THAT YOUR EYES GO WHERE YOU WANT, AND YOUR AUDIENCE WILL DO THE SAME.

FINALLY, I WANT TO TALK ABOUT ***PROPORTIONS.*** THE AVERAGE PERSON IS 7.5 HEADS HIGH. THIS MEANS THAT IF YOU TOOK THE HEIGHT OF A PERSON'S HEAD AND STACKED THEM SEVEN AND A HALF TIMES, THAT'S ABOUT HOW TALL THEY WOULD BE. PLAYING WITH THIS RULE HAS RECOGNIZABLE EFFECTS. MAKING A PERSON 8 OR 8.5 HEADS HIGH (LIKE THE EXAMPLE ON THE RIGHT) MAKES THE SUBJECT LOOK STRONGER AND MORE HEROIC. GO DOWN IN SIZE TO 7 OR 6.5 HEADS HIGH AND THE EFFECT GOES THE OTHER WAY: STOCKY, PUDGY, AND POSSIBLY EVEN WEAK.

NO RULES ARE SET IN STONE, BUT ALL PRINCIPLES MUST BE KEPT IN MIND. BE SURE TO PRACTICE THESE AS YOU DRAW, AND MAKE SURE TO HAVE FUN!

ABINADI

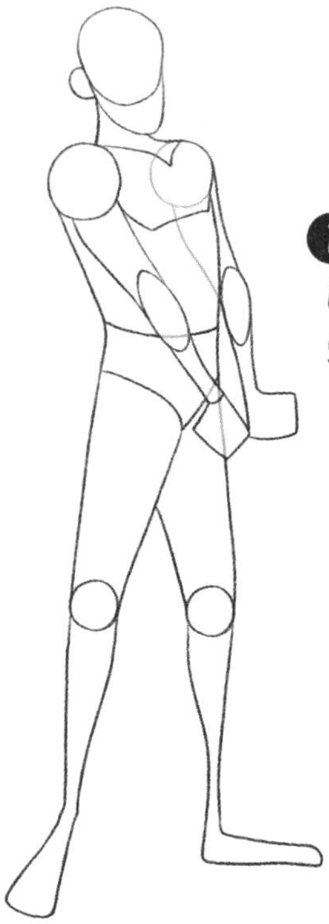

❶ BLOCK IN THE SHAPES. EVEN THOUGH ABINADI IS IN CHAINS, HAVING HIS CHEST HIGH AND PUFFED OUT STILL GIVES HIM A FEELING OF STRENGTH AND POWER.

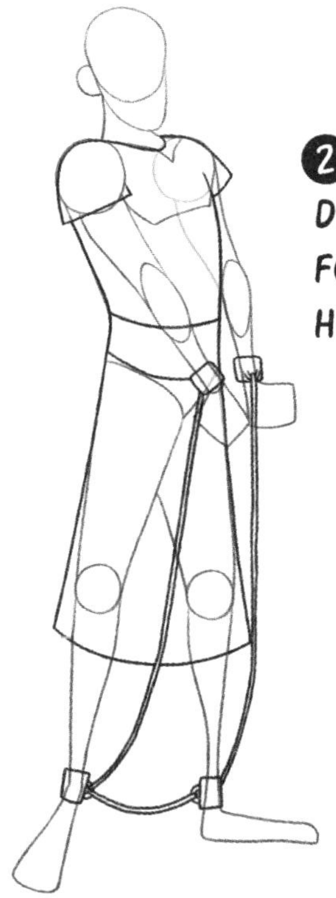

❷ DRAW IN THE CLOTHES. WE'LL PUT DETAIL IN THE CHAINS LATER, BUT FOR NOW MAKE SURE THAT IT HANGS THE RIGHT WAY.

❸ DEFINE FORMS. REMEMBER TO USE THE STRAIGHTS AGAINST CURVES PRINCIPLE TO MAKE THE ARM MORE INTERESTING (JUST DON'T OVERDO IT SO IT DOESN'T LOOK WEIRD).

❹ PUT IN THE DETAILS. NOW YOU CAN DRAW IN THE REST OF THE CHAIN. I ALSO TATTERED HIS CLOTHES TO TELL MORE OF THE STORY IN JUST ONE DRAWING.

❺ BLOCK IN COLOR OR BLACK. SINCE ABINADI IS A PRISONER IN THIS DRAWING, KEEP THE COLORING SIMPLE. THAT'S ANOTHER EASY THING THAT CAN FURTHER TELL THE STORY.

ABISH

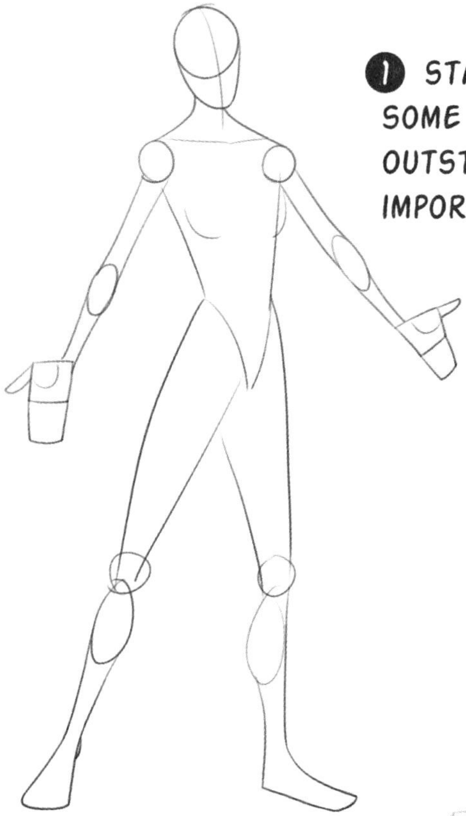

❶ START BY BLOCKING IN SHAPES. AGAIN, WE WANT TO PUT SOME PERSONALITY IN THE POSE. THE WIDE STANCE AND OUTSTRETCHED ARMS SUGGEST SHE IS SAYING SOMETHING IMPORTANT WITH POWER.

❷ DRAW CLOTHES, SANDALS, AND ACCESSORIES OVER BLOCKED-IN SHAPES. REMEMBER, IF THE CLOTHES ARE RESTING ON THE BODY OR UNDER BELTS, THEY SHOULD BE TIGHTER TO THE BODY.

❸ DEFINE FORMS. YOU'LL NOTICE I SPLIT ONE OF THE FINGERS APART FROM THE REST. THOUGH I LIKE TO KEEP THINGS SIMPLE, FINGERS ARE RARELY ALL TOGETHER, AND IT MAKES A MORE INTERESTING SHAPE.

❹ ADD IN HAIR AND DETAILS. THE HAIR SHOULD SIT A BIT ABOVE THE HEAD AND FALL DOWN AT THE SIDES. REMEMBER WHERE THE FOLDS IN THE CLOTHES SHOULD GO, ESPECIALLY BY THE ARMPITS AND WAIST.

PEOPLE ALWAYS LOOK AT THE FACE FIRST, SO FRAMING THE FACE BY DARKENING THE HAIR CALLS MORE ATTENTION.

❺ COLOR IN SOME ACCENTS. THIS STEP IS OPTIONAL, BUT I'LL ALWAYS RECOMMEND IT BECAUSE IT BREAKS UP THE FORMS AND MAKES IT MORE INTERESTING. YOU ALSO DON'T HAVE TO FILL IN WHERE I DID. TRY DIFFERENT THINGS AND SEE WHAT YOU LIKE BEST.

ALMA

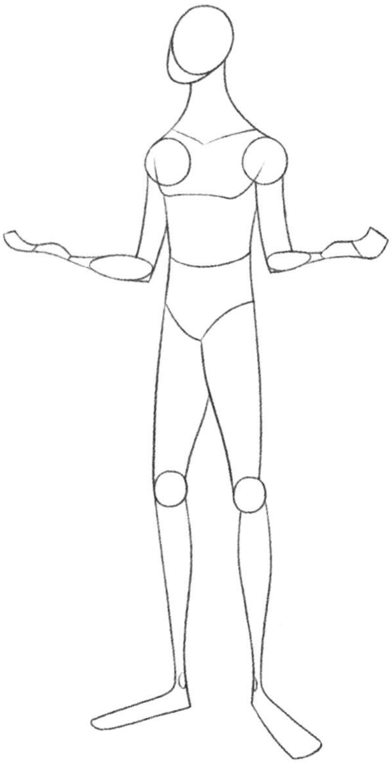

❶ BLOCK IN THE SHAPES. DON'T BE AFRAID TO EXAGGERATE OR TRY SOMETHING NEW. WE'LL TRY STRETCHING OUT THE NECK. REMEMBER, IF YOU TRY SOMETHING NEW AND DON'T LIKE IT, YOU CAN ALWAYS GO BACK AND CHANGE IT, BUT YOU MAY FIND SOMETHING NEW THAT WORKS.

❷ DRAW IN THE CLOTHES OVER THE FORMS. EVEN THOUGH THE HAT WOULDN'T SIT LIKE THAT ON HIS NECK/SHOULDER, WE'LL LEAVE IT TO KEEP THE NICE FLOW THROUGH THE LINE.

❸ DEFINE ALL THE FORMS. ALTHOUGH I THINK THE LONG NECK LOOKS FINE, I GAVE HIM A BEARD JUST FOR LOOKS. ALSO, BEARDS CAN MAKE CHARACTERS LOOK MORE WISE.

❹ DRAW THE DETAILS.

❺ BLOCK IN COLOR OR BLACK. I WENT BACK AND FORTH AS TO WHICH PARTS TO DARKEN; I DID TWO VERSIONS AND BOTH LOOKED GOOD. REMEMBER AS YOU GO THROUGH THIS BOOK, THERE IS NO ONE ANSWER OR ONE WAY TO DO THINGS. BE SURE TO TRY DIFFERENT THINGS FROM WHAT I DO AND HAVE FUN.

AMMON

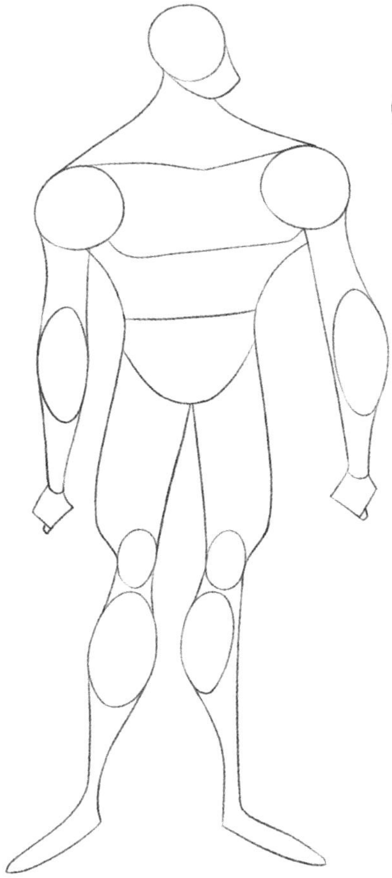

❶ BLOCK IN THE SHAPES. WE'LL PUSH SHAPES A BIT IN THIS ONE, SPECIFICALLY IN THE FEET. INSTEAD OF DRAWING THEM SQUARED OFF, WE'LL KEEP THEM ROUND TO SHOW THAT AS LONG AS THE SHAPE IS RIGHT, AND THEY ARE IN THE RIGHT PLACE, THEY DON'T HAVE TO BE EXACT.

❷ DRAW CLOTHES AND SHEATH OVER SHAPES.

❸ DEFINE FORMS. REMEMBER THE STRAIGHTS AGAINST CURVES PRINCIPLE. I HIGHLIGHTED A COUPLE OF THEM JUST TO SHOW WHERE IT HAS BEEN USED.

❹ DRAW IN THE SWORD AND SMALL DETAILS. REMEMBER TO DRAW WRINKLES WHERE THE CLOTHES SIT. SINCE HIS CAPE ATTACHES OVER HIS CHEST, THAT'S WHERE A BIT OF STRETCHING WOULD HAPPEN. ALSO, CLOTHES TEND TO BUNCH UP UNDERNEATH THINGS LIKE BELTS.

❺ FILL IN AREAS WITH BLACK (OR WHATEVER COLOR YOU PREFER). THE OVERALL SHAPE IS MORE INTERESTING WHEN BREAKING THINGS UP WITH COLOR, BUT BE SURE TO SPREAD IT OUT OVER DIFFERENT PARTS. CREATING BANDS OF COLOR INSTEAD OF BUNCHING IT ALL TOGETHER HELPS THE OVERALL LOOK.

AMULEK

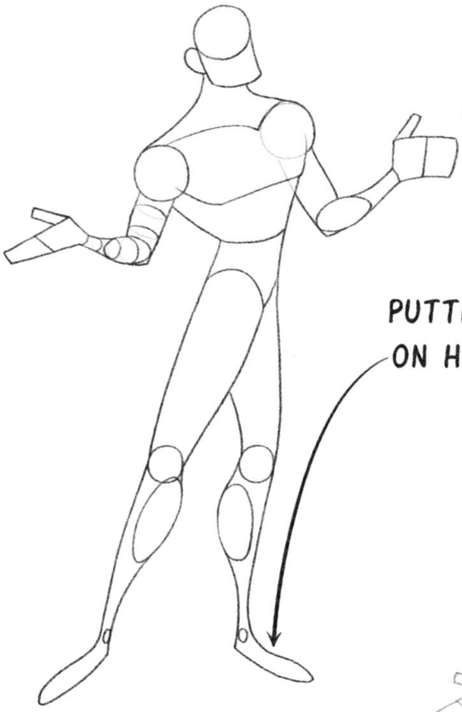

❶ BLOCK IN THE SHAPES. I PUT THE RINGS ON HIS RIGHT ARM TO SHOW FORESHORTENING SO YOU CAN SEE THAT ONE ARM ISN'T LONGER THAN THE OTHER.

PUTTING A CHARACTER HEAVILY ON HIS FRONT FOOT IS A GOOD CONFIDENT POSE.

❷ DRAW CLOTHES OVER THE FORM.

❸ DEFINE THE FORMS. I LIKE TO EXAGGERATE FEATURES TO REALLY MAKE THEM STAND OUT. I WANT AMULEK TO LOOK STRONG, SO I REALLY NARROWED HIS WAIST TO MAKE EVERYTHING ELSE APPEAR WIDER.

4 DRAW IN ALL THE DETAILS. I LOVE DRAWING HANDS; THEY HAVE GREAT LINES AND CAN BE SO EXPRESSIVE. IF YOU LOOK AT HIS RIGHT HAND AND THINK IT LOOKS DIFFICULT, THAT'S OKAY! JUST MAKE SURE TO PRACTICE AS MUCH AS YOU CAN.

5 FILL IN AREAS WITH BLACK OR COLOR. I'LL SAY THIS AGAIN AND AGAIN: UNLESS YOU HAVE A SPECIFIC AREA YOU WANT TO HIGHLIGHT WITH CONTRAST, IT IS OFTEN BEST TO CREATE A STRIPED PATTERN OF DARK, LIGHT, DARK.

BROTHER OF JARED

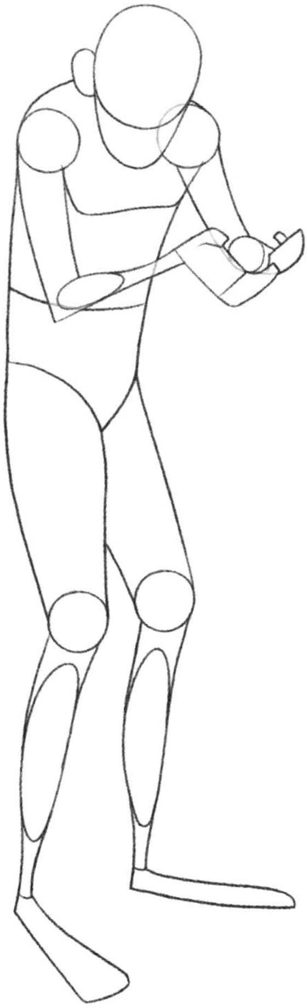

❶ BLOCK IN THE SHAPES. REALLY, NO ONE WOULD HAVE THEIR SHOULDERS PULLED UP THAT HIGH, BUT IF YOU WANT YOUR CHARACTER TO SHOW A SPECIFIC EMOTION, IT IS BEST TO OVERDO IT RATHER THAN NOT SHOW ENOUGH.

❷ DRAW CLOTHES OVER THE FORM. CLOTH WILL ALWAYS FALL STRAIGHT DOWN UNLESS SOMETHING GETS IN THE WAY. THIS CAN BE USED TO CREATE NICE STRAIGHTS AND CURVES.

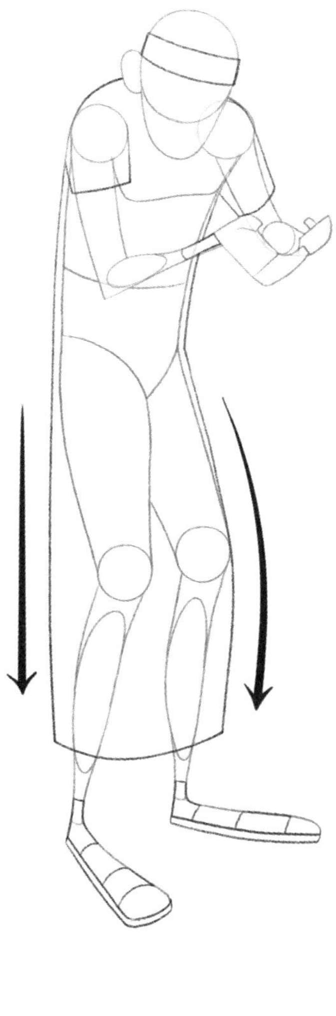

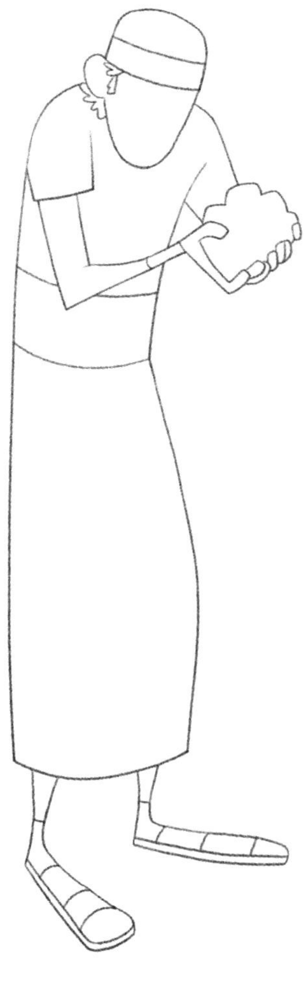

❸ DEFINE THE FORMS. EVEN THOUGH THE LEFT ARM GETS COVERED UP BY THE STONES IN HIS HANDS, IT IS ALWAYS IMPORTANT TO DRAW THE WHOLE FORM FIRST TO MAKE SURE EVERYTHING IS IN THE RIGHT PLACE.

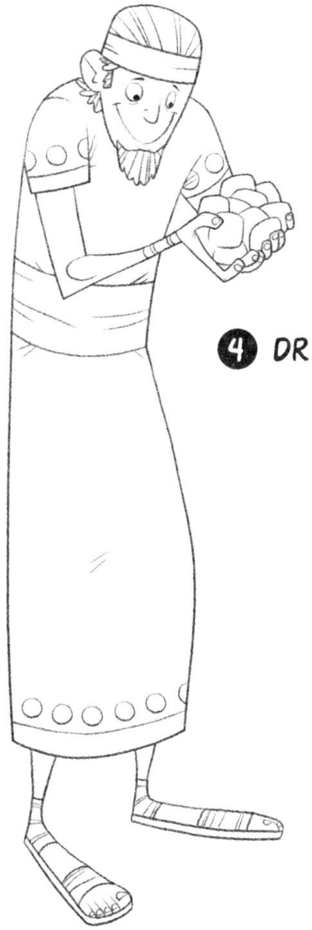

❹ DRAW IN ALL THE SMALL DETAILS.

❺ FILL IN AREAS WITH BLACK OR COLOR. ADDING LINES OUTSIDE THE STONES HELPS TO SHOW THAT THEY ARE GIVING OFF LIGHT AND THAT HE IS NOT HOLDING JUST A PILE OF ROCKS.

CAPTAIN MORONI

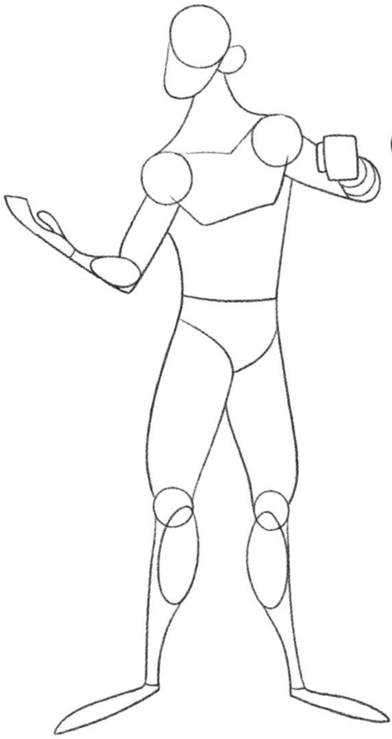

❶ BLOCK IN THE SHAPES. NOTICE THE RINGS AROUND HIS LEFT ARM. THIS IS TO SHOW **FORESHORTENING.** REFER BACK TO PAGE 7 IF YOU NEED HELP.

❷ DRAW CLOTHES AND ARMOR OVER THE FORM.

❸ DEFINE THE FORMS. EVEN THOUGH THE HELMET IS NOT ON HIS HEAD, I THINK HAVING IT IN THE DRAWING COMPLETES THE WHOLE LOOK AND FEEL.

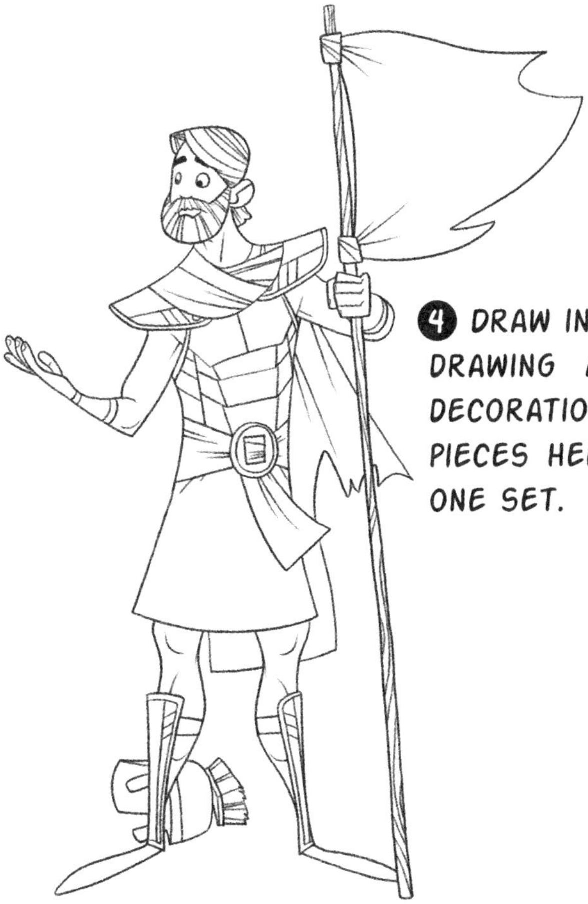

❹ DRAW IN ALL THE SMALL DETAILS. PART OF THE FUN IN DRAWING ARMOR IS THE DECORATION. KEEPING THE DECORATIONS THE SAME THROUGHOUT THE DIFFERENT PIECES HELPS THEM FEEL LIKE THEY ARE ALL PART OF ONE SET.

❺ FILL IN AREAS WITH BLACK OR COLOR.

ENOS

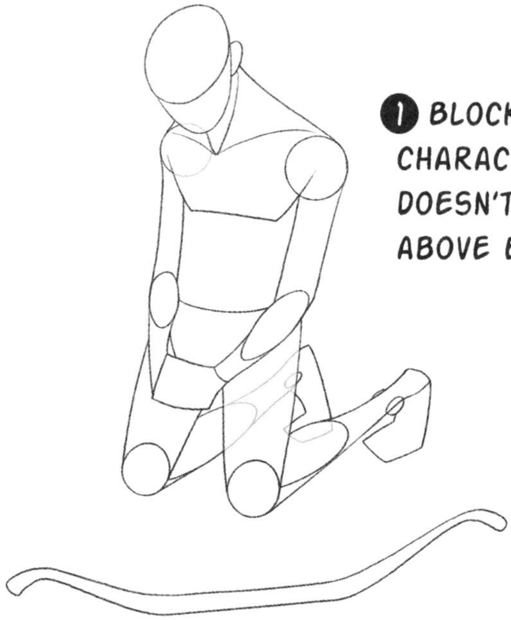

❶ BLOCK IN THE SHAPES. WE WANT TO SHOW HUMILITY IN THIS CHARACTER, SO HIS BODY STAYS WITHIN ONE SHAPE AND DOESN'T BREAK OUTSIDE OF IT. LOOKING DOWN AT HIM FROM ABOVE ENHANCES THE FEELING.

❷ DRAW CLOTHES OVER THE FORM. DRAWING THE WHOLE BACK LEG IN STEP 1 HELPS YOU KNOW WHERE THE CLOTHES SHOULD SIT.

❸ DEFINE THE FORMS.

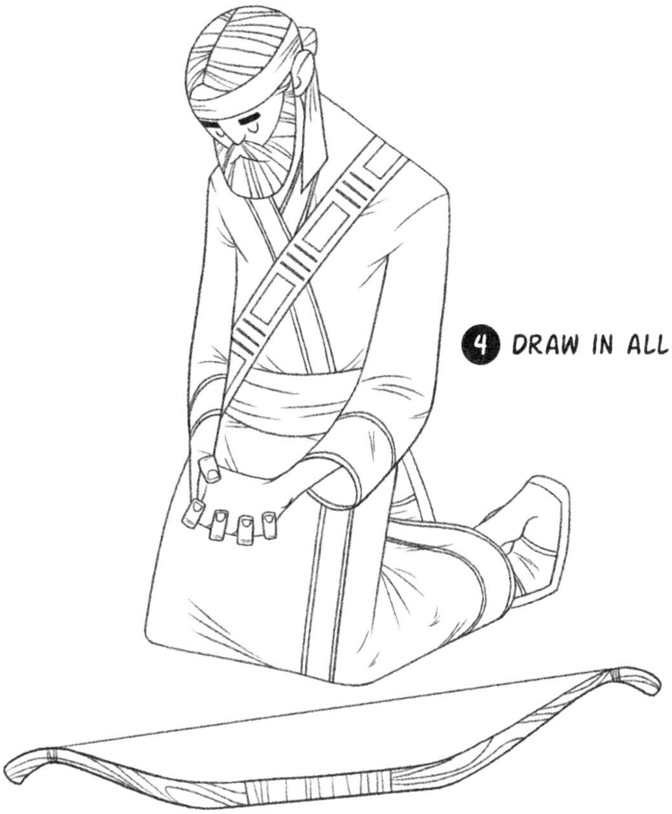

❹ DRAW IN ALL THE DETAILS. BE SURE NOT TO FORGET THE BOW!

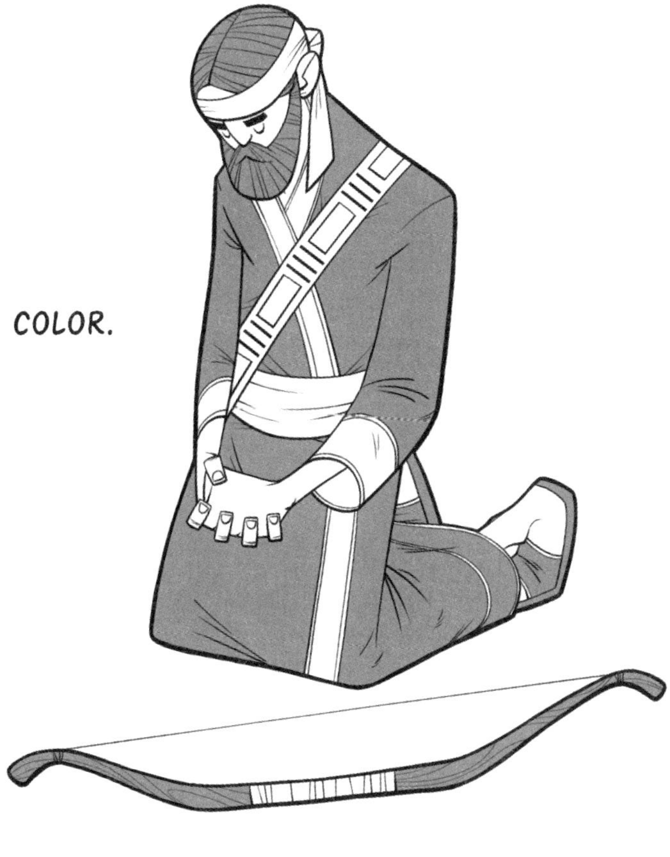

❺ FILL IN AREAS WITH BLACK OR COLOR.

GADIANTON

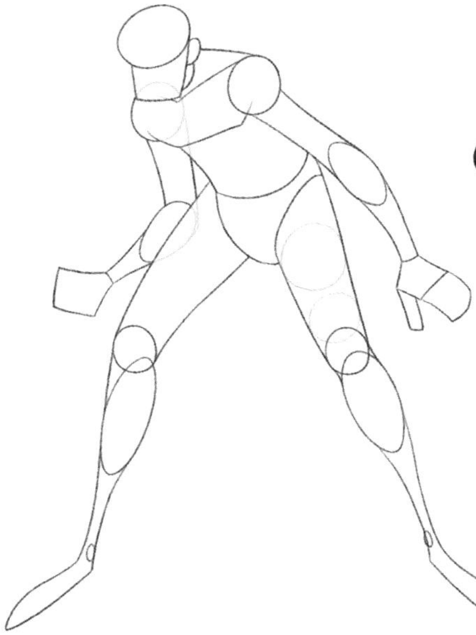

❶ BLOCK IN THE SHAPES. KEEPING THE HEAD LOW CAN MEAN A FEW DIFFERENT THINGS. IN THIS DRAWING, THE LOWERED HEAD, ALONG WITH THE OVERALL POSE, GIVES A FEELING OF SNEAKINESS OR SHADINESS.

❷ DRAW CLOTHES OVER THE FORM. GIVING HIM A SWINGING CAPE ADDS A BIT OF DRAMA AND MOVEMENT.

❸ DEFINE THE FORMS. NOTICE WHAT I DID WITH THE HANDS. JUST AS WITH ABISH, I SEPARATED THE FINGERS; KEEPING THEM ALL TOGETHER WOULD MAKE HIM FEEL ROBOTIC.

❹ DRAW IN ALL THE DETAILS.

❺ FILL IN AREAS WITH BLACK OR COLOR. THE CAPE IS A NICE WAY TO FRAME OBJECTS. YOU CAN'T DRAW ONE ON EVERYBODY, SO USE IT WHILE YOU CAN!

GIDEON

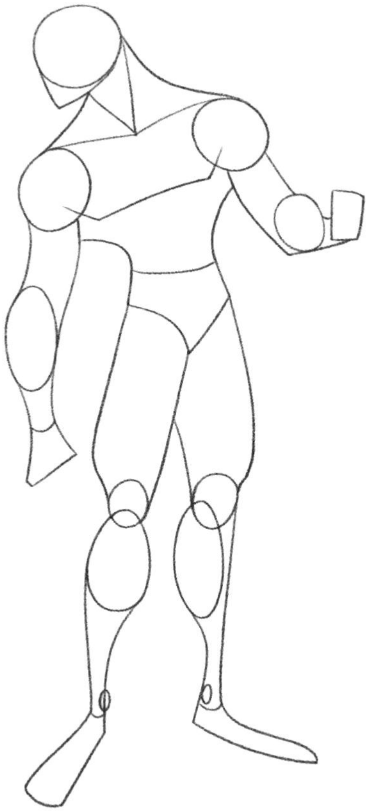

1 BLOCK IN THE SHAPES. I LIKE TO CHANGE UP BODY SHAPES TO KEEP THINGS INTERESTING. THICK NECK, BROAD SHOULDERS, NARROW WAIST, AND LONG LEGS ARE CHARACTERSTIC OF A "HEROIC" LOOK.

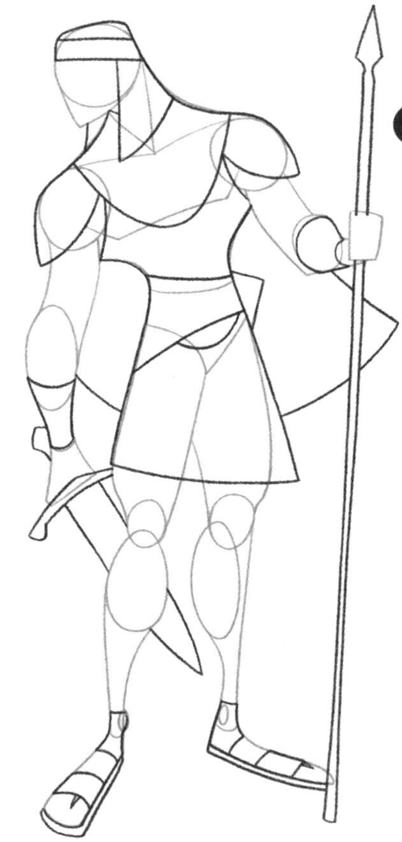

2 DRAW CLOTHES AND ARMOR OVER THE FORM. CONTINUING THE HERO THEME, I GAVE HIM A SWORD AND A SPEAR. BOTH ARE OPTIONAL, SO MAKE IT YOURS!

3 DEFINE THE FORMS. WHEN LOOKING FROM THE SIDE, THE BRIDGE OF THE NOSE DOESN'T ACTUALLY COME STRAIGHT DOWN FROM THE FOREHEAD LIKE I HAVE DRAWN HERE, BUT DOING SO IS ANOTHER THING THAT PORTRAYS STRENGTH.

NOTICE THE EYEBROWS. WE AUTOMOTICALLY LOOK AT THE FACE FIRST, SO BE SURE YOUR DRAWING PORTRAYS WHAT YOU WANT. EYEBROWS ANGLED UP (/ \) SHOW WORRY OR SADNESS, FLAT EYEBROWS (— —) SHOW DETERMINATION OR SERIOUSNESS, AND EYEBROWS ANGLED DOWN (\ /) SHOW ANGER.

4 DRAW IN ALL THE DETAILS.

5 FILL IN AREAS WITH BLACK OR COLOR. I LIKE TO MAKE SURE SOMETHING AT THE TOP AND BOTTOM ARE BOTH COLORED OR DARKENED. THIS ACTS AS SORT OF A WALL TO KEEP YOUR EYES FROM LEAVING THE IMAGE.

HELAMAN

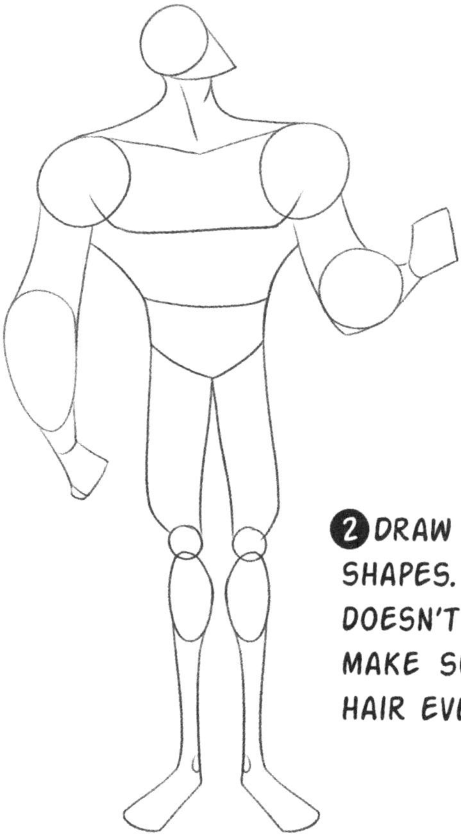

❶ BLOCK IN THE SHAPES. I LIKE TO SWITCH UP MY STYLE SOMETIMES TO KEEP THINGS FUN AND INTERESTING. PART OF THE FUN OF DRAWING IS PLAYING WITH SHAPES AND SIZES. WITH HELAMAN, WE WILL HAVE A LITTLE FUN WITH PROPORTIONS. MAKING THE HEAD SMALLER AND THE SHOULDERS WIDER IT GIVES THE APPEARANCE OF GREAT STRENGTH.

❷ DRAW CLOTHES AND ARMOR OVER SHAPES. NOTICE THAT THE HELMET DOESN'T SIT RIGHT ON THE HEAD. MAKE SURE TO ACCOUNT FOR THE HAIR EVEN IF YOU CAN'T SEE IT.

SOMEONE LIKE THIS WOULDN'T HAVE WRISTS THIS TINY, BUT IT MAKES HIS MUSCLES LOOK EVEN BIGGER AND CREATES FUN SHAPES.

❸ DEFINE FORMS. YOU'VE PROBABLY NOTICED THAT I END UP DRAWING HIM WITH A BEARD. DRAWING THE FACE FIRST IS HELPFUL TO MAKE SURE EVERYTHING SITS WHERE IT SHOULD.

❹ I DON'T PUT IN THE DETAILS UNTIL I LIKE ALL THE SHAPES FROM THE PREVIOUS STEP. ONCE THAT HAPPENS, I USUALLY DON'T BREAK OUTSIDE OF THOSE LINES. THE OBVIOUS EXCEPTION IS HIS SPEAR. DRAW IN THE FINGERS, TOES, A FEW LINES TO SHOW WHERE MUSCLES ARE, AND SOME FOLDS IN THE CLOTHES. AS ALWAYS, YOU DON'T HAVE TO FOLLOW EXACTLY WHAT I HAVE DONE, ESPECIALLY ON THE ARMOR. TRY DRAWING DIFFERENT DESIGNS!

❺ NOW IT IS TIME TO DECIDE WHAT TO FILL IN BLACK AND WHAT TO LEAVE WHITE. IT IS ALWAYS A GOOD IDEA TO SPREAD APART THE BLACK BLOCKS OF COLOR. NOTICE ON HELAMAN THAT THE BLACK SECTIONS ARE AT THE VERY TOP, THE MIDDLE, AND THE BOTTOM. IT IS NOT ALWAYS NECESSARY, BUT IT'S GENERALLY A GOOD IDEA.

KING NOAH

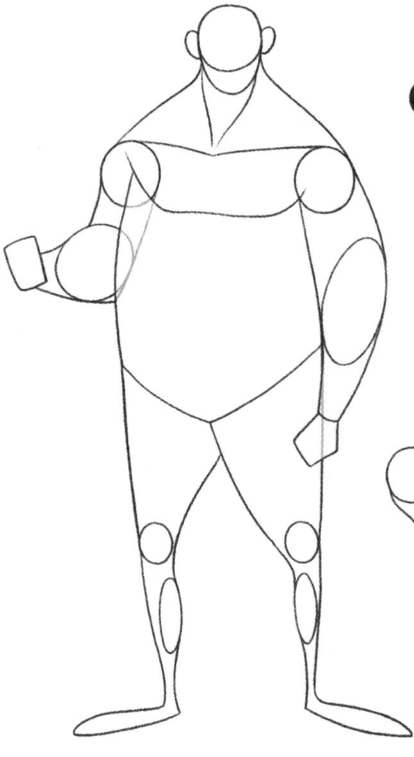

❶ BLOCK IN THE SHAPES. I GRAYED OUT SOME OF THE OVERLAPPING LINES ON HIS RIGHT ARM. THIS IS TO SHOW THAT EVEN THOUGH THAT PART WON'T BE SEEN, YOU SHOULD STILL DRAW IT TO MAKE SURE EVERYTHING IS WHERE IT SHOULD BE.

❷ DRAW CLOTHES OVER THE FORM. SINCE NOAH WAS A KING, WE'LL GIVE HIM A LOT OF EXTRA CLOTHES THAT WILL COME TOGETHER AS WE GO THROUGH THE STEPS.

❸ DEFINE THE FORMS.

❹ DRAW IN THE DETAILS. MAKE SURE TO TAKE TIME ON THIS STEP. WE WANT HIM TO LOOK LIKE A KING WHO LOVES EXPENSIVE THINGS LIKE GOLD AND SILVER. BE SURE TO ADD A LOT OF SMALL DECORATIONS, JEWELS, AND THINGS LIKE THAT.

❺ FILL IN AREAS WITH BLACK OR COLOR. IF YOU COLOR YOUR DRAWING, REMEMBER THAT BLUES AND PURPLES WERE THE MOST EXPENSIVE AND RARE FABRIC COLORS AT THAT TIME, AND SO THEY WERE OFTEN USED BY ROYALTY.

LAMAN

❶ BLOCK IN SHAPES. WHEN COMPARED TO NEPHI, YOU CAN SEE THAT HIS HIPS ARE WIDER AND HIS MIDSECTION IS THICKER. THIS TENDS TO HAPPEN AS PEOPLE GET OLDER, AND I LIKE TO THINK THAT, EVEN THOUGH LAMAN IS A BIGGER GUY, NEPHI STILL HAS AN EDGE ON HIM.

❷ DRAW CLOTHES AND SANDALS OVER BLOCKED-IN SHAPES.

IF YOU EVER HAVE TROUBLE POSITIONING THE FEET, BLOCK IN WHERE THE SOLES OF THE SHOES SHOULD BE AND DRAW UP FROM THERE.

❸ DEFINE FORMS. YOU DON'T HAVE TO FOLLOW YOUR PREVIOUS LINES. YOU MAY FIND THAT A DIFFERENT ANGLE OR POSITION LOOKS BETTER. IT'S EASIER TO FIX IT NOW RATHER THAN WHEN IT'S ALL FINISHED.

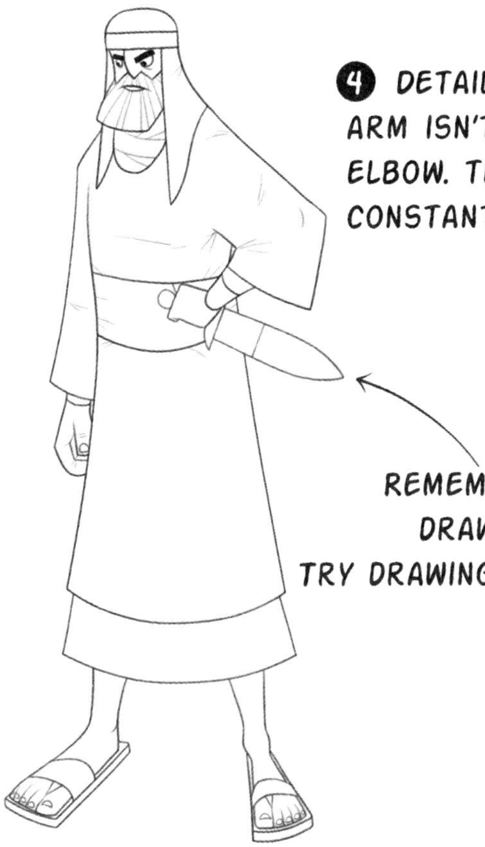

4 DETAILS (AND SWORD) TIME! EVEN THOUGH HIS RIGHT ARM ISN'T BENT, I STILL PUT THE FOLDS AT ABOUT THE ELBOW. THERE ARE USUALLY STILL CREASES THERE FROM CONSTANT BENDING.

REMEMBER, YOU DON'T HAVE TO DRAW EXACTLY WHAT I DO. TRY DRAWING SOMETHING DIFFERENT HERE!

5 GO AHEAD AND FINISH IT OFF BY ADDING COLOR OR BLOCK IN SOME AREAS WITH BLACK. YOU CAN EVEN EXPERIMENT WITH SIMPLE BACKGROUNDS OR EVEN JUST PUT SOME ROCKS NEXT TO HIS FEET SO HE'S NOT FLOATING ON THE PAGE.

LEHI

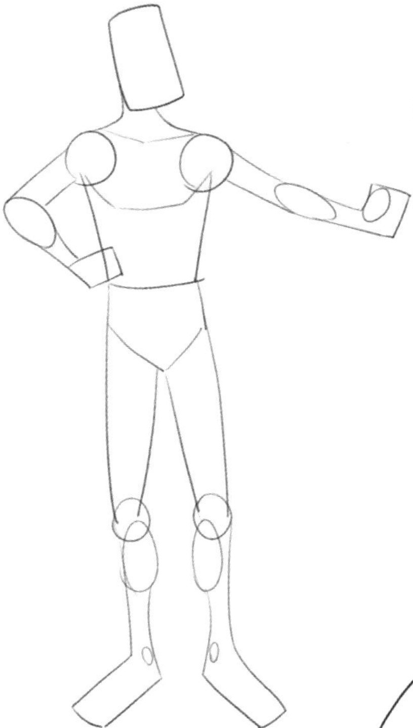

❶ BLOCK IN THE SHAPES. IT'S A SMALL THING, BUT SINCE HIS RIGHT ARM IS ON HIS HIP AND HIS LEFT HAND WILL BE HOLDING A STAFF, HIS SHOULDERS WILL BE A BIT HIGHER WITHOUT HAVING TO SUPPORT THE WEIGHT OF HIS ARMS HANGING DOWN.

❷ DRAW CLOTHES AND SANDALS OVER BLOCKED-IN SHAPES. REMEMBER THAT ANY SORT OF HAT WILL SIT ON TOP OF THE HAIR NOT THE HEAD, SO BE SURE TO LEAVE SOME EXTRA ROOM BETWEEN THE HAT AND THE HEAD SHAPE.

I DIDN'T TOTALLY FOLLOW THE FORM UNDERNEATH FOR THE SHOULDERS. I DID THIS TO KEEP THE FLOW FROM HIS HEAD DOWN TO HIS ARMS.

❸ DEFINE FORMS. LET'S PUT THE STAFF IN HIS HAND NOW SO WE KNOW WHERE TO PUT THE FINGERS THAT WRAP AROUND.

❹ DETAILS, DETAILS, DETAILS. WHENEVER I DRAW WOOD OR TREES, I LIKE TO ADD LINES AS WOOD GRAIN. KIND OF LIKE THE LINES IN THE BEARD, IT GIVES THE OBJECT SOME INTEREST, VARIETY, AND TEXTURE.

LITTLE DETAILS SUCH AS WHAT I PUT ON THE SANDAL STRAPS CAN BE DRAWN ANYWHERE ON CLOTHES TO MAKE THEM A BIT MORE INTERESTING.

❺ BLOCK IN COLOR OR BLACK. USUALLY I WOULD DARKEN THE BEARD TO FRAME THE FACE, BUT REMEMBER THAT KEEPING THE BEARD WHITE SHOWS HIS AGE BETTER.

LEMUEL

❶ BLOCK IN SHAPES. THINGS GET A LITTLE CRAZY AROUND THE ARMS AND CHEST, BUT IT'S IMPORTANT TO DRAW EVERYTHING EVEN IF BODY PARTS ARE OVERLAPPING, THAT WAY YOU CAN BE SURE EVERYTHING IS THE RIGHT SIZE. ARMS AND LEGS CAN EASILY END UP LOOKING WEIRD WITHOUT DOING THIS.

BODY POSTURE IS IMPORTANT. EVEN THOUGH HE IS A BIG GUY, HIS CLOSED AND NARROW STANCE MAKES HIM FEEL UNSTEADY.

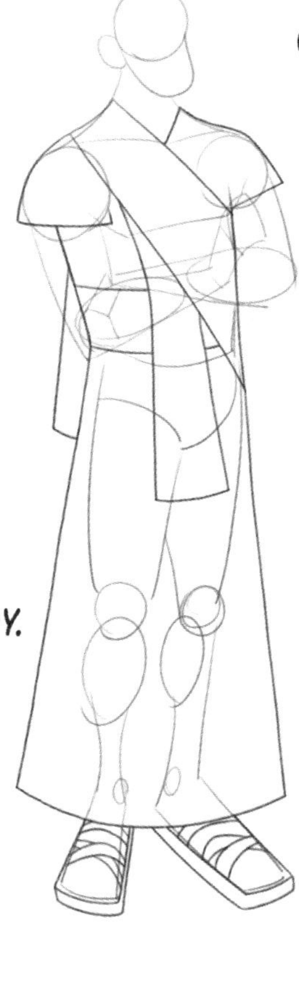

❷ DRAW CLOTHES AND SANDALS OVER BLOCKED-IN SHAPES. JUST LIKE THE PREVIOUS STEP, EVEN THOUGH YOU WON'T SEE THE ALL THE CLOTHES. STILL DRAW THEM UNDERNEATH THE ARMS TO MAKE SURE EVERYTHING MATCHES UP.

❸ DEFINE FORMS. REMEMBER THAT HAIR AND BEARD SIT ON THE HEAD AND FACE, SO IT'S HELPFUL TO DRAW THE FORM UNDERNEATH FIRST.

4 DETAILS. THE IMPORTANT THINGS ARE FINGERS, TOES, FACIAL FEATURES, HAIR, FOLDS OF THE CLOTHES—THINGS THAT GENERALLY EVERYONE HAS. I LIKE TO ADD THINGS LIKE THE LINES N THE HAIR AND BEARD TO DESCRIBE THE FLOW BECAUSE I FEEL IT LOOKS GOOD. REMEMBER, YOU ARE ALWAYS FREE TO TRY SOMETHING ELSE. MAKE THIS YOUR OWN.

5 THE ALWAYS OPTIONAL STEP OF BLOCKING IN EITHER BLACK OR COLOR. DON'T PUT THE BLACK ALL IN THE SAME AREA. IT'S BEST TO PATTERN IT (BACK, WHITE, BLACK, WHITE) IF POSSIBLE.

MORMON

❶ BLOCK IN THE SHAPES. NOTICE THE RINGS AROUND HIS LEFT ARM AND REMEMBER THE TIP FROM PAGE 7 ABOUT FORESHORTENING. USE THE RINGS TO HELP OUT WITH PLACEMENT.

❷ DRAW CLOTHES OVER THE FORMS. SINCE THE PAPER IS SUCH A BIG PART OF THIS DRAWING, I DREW THAT FIRST AND THE CLOTHES UNDERNEATH.

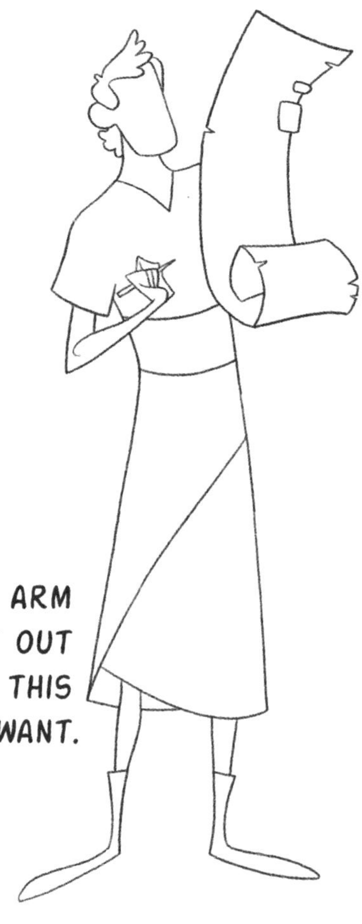

❸ DEFINE FORMS. EVEN THOUGH YOU COULD SEE PART OF HIS ARM STICKING OUT FROM BEHIND THE PAPER IN STEP 2, I TOOK IT OUT BECAUSE I FELT IT WASN'T NECESSARY. AS YOU GO THROUGH THIS BOOK, FEEL FREE TO CHANGE, ADD, OR REMOVE ANYTHING YOU WANT.

WE SPLIT APART THE TOP FINGER IN STEP 3. IF YOU HOLD SOMETHING UP IN FRONT OF YOU YOU WILL NOTICE THAT ALL OF YOUR FINGERS DON'T STAY TOGETHER. REMEMBER THIS ANY TIME YOU DRAW HANDS.

4. DRAW IN ALL THE SMALL DETAILS.

5. FILL IN AREAS WITH BLACK OR COLOR. WHETHER YOU PUT IN A LOT OF BLACK, LIKE I DID, OR JUST A LITTLE, BE SURE YOU DO IT TO BREAK UP THE FIGURE. THE DARKS AND LIGHTS SHOULD LOOK ALMOST LIKE STRIPES.

MORONI

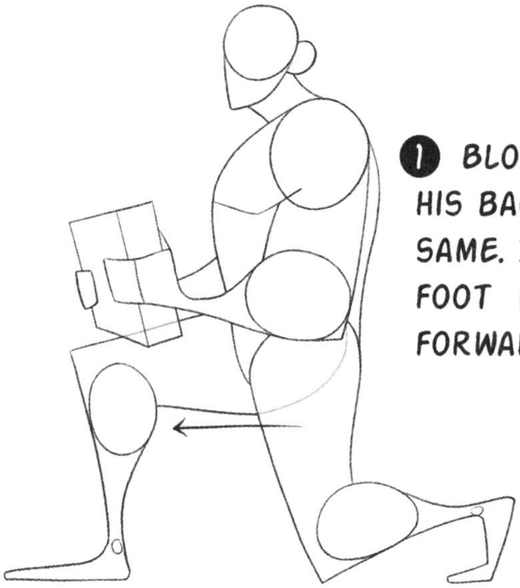

❶ BLOCK IN THE SHAPES. MAKE SURE TO DRAW THROUGH ON HIS BACK LEG SO THAT THE LENGTH OF BOTH LEGS ARE THE SAME. I DREW IN THE ARROW TO SHOW THAT SINCE HIS RIGHT FOOT IS SO FAR FORWARD, HIS WHOLE LEG WILL SHIFT FORWARD.

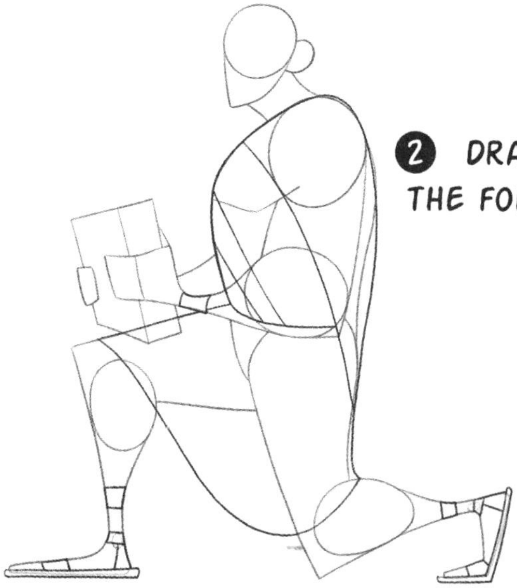

❷ DRAW IN THE CLOTHES OVER THE FORMS.

❸ DEFINE FORMS. I LIKE CAPES. I FEEL IT ALWAYS MAKES A CHARACTER LOOK MORE DRAMATIC WITH IT BLOWING IN THE WIND. IN THIS CASE, HOWEVER, WE WILL USE IT TO FRAME THE PLATES HE HIS HOLDING AND MAKE THEM STAND OUT BY DARKENING THE CAPE IN STEP 5.

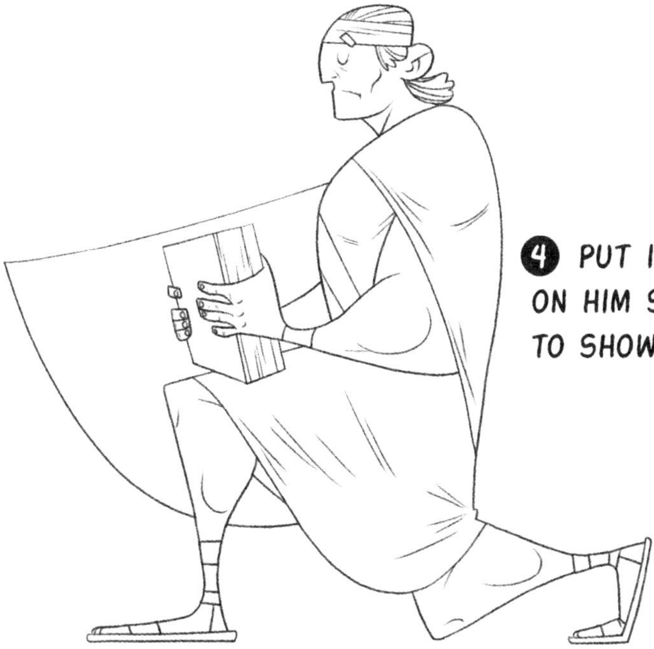

4 PUT IN THE DETAILS. SINCE THE CLOTHES SIT ON HIM SO CLOSELY, BE SURE TO USE THE FOLDS TO SHOW WHERE THE FORMS ARE UNDERNEATH.

5 BLOCK IN COLOR OR BLACK. LIKE I SAID IN STEP 3, YOU CAN USE COLOR TO CALL ATTENTION TO SPECIFIC PARTS OF YOUR DRAWING. HERE I'VE DARKENED ALMOST EVERYTHING AROUND THE PLATES TO DRAW YOUR EYES THERE.

NEPHI

❶ BLOCK IN THE SHAPES. WHEN I THINK OF NEPHI, I THINK OF BOLD AND STRONG. TO CONVEY THAT, WE'LL PUT HIS CHEST AND CHIN HIGH, FEET PLANTED WIDE, AND HANDS ON HIS HIPS IN A HEROIC POSE.

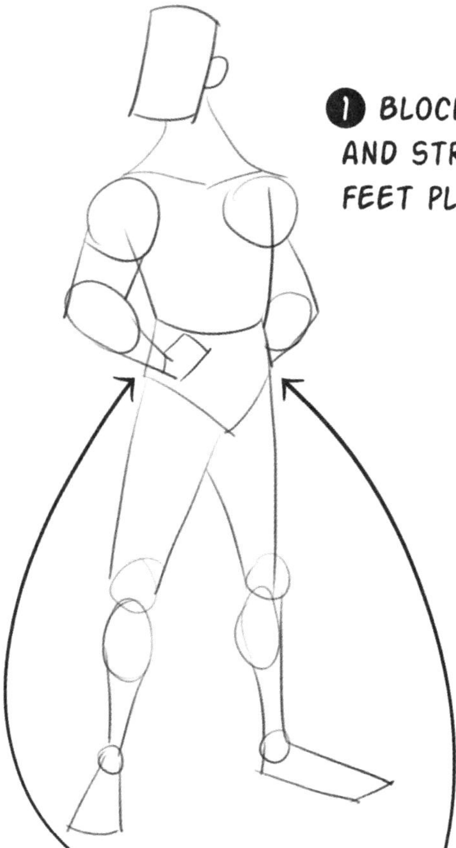

OVERLAPPING BODY PARTS GIVE THE FIGURE MORE DEPTH.

❷ DRAW CLOTHES AND SANDALS OVER BLOCKED-IN SHAPES. IT'S IMPORTANT TO DRAW THE WHOLE BODY FIRST TO KNOW WHERE THE CLOTHES SHOULD SIT.

❸ DEFINE FORMS. SAVE THE SMALLER DETAILS FOR LATER. IT'S NOT FUN TO SPEND TIME ON DETAILS ONLY TO ERASE IT ALL WHEN YOU FIND OUT THE OVERALL FORM DOESN'T LOOK RIGHT.

4 NOW IT'S TIME FOR DETAILS. I LIKE TO KEEP THINGS SIMPLE, ESPECIALLY WITH HANDS AND FEET. I USUALLY DON'T BREAK OUTSIDE THE BASIC FORM I'VE ALREADY DRAWN; I JUST ADD IN THE TOES, KNUCKLES, AND OTHER LITTLE THINGS. ALSO NOTE THE FOLDS I'VE PUT IN THE CLOTHES NEAR THE SHOULDERS AND HIS "BELT." THIS IS ANOTHER DETAIL THAT DESCRIBES FORM A LITTLE BETTER.

I DECIDED TO BREAK UP THE SHAPE AND HAVE THE FLAP HANG DOWN. THAT'S HOW THESE CLOTHES WOULD NATURALLY FALL.

5 FILLING IN DIFFERENT AREAS WITH BLACK WILL MAKE THE CHARACTER POP WITH SOME CONTRAST AND BREAKS UP THE OVERALL SHAPE.

SAMUEL THE LAMANITE

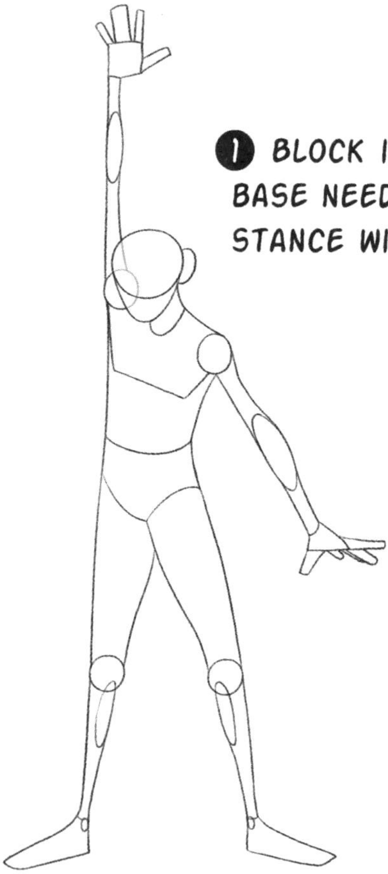

❶ BLOCK IN THE SHAPES. THE TALLER THE FIGURE IS, THE WIDER THE BASE NEEDS TO BE. SINCE HIS ARM MAKES HIM LONGER, WE'LL MAKE HIS STANCE WIDE AND HIS FEET SPREAD APART.

❷ DRAW IN THE CLOTHES OVER THE FORMS.

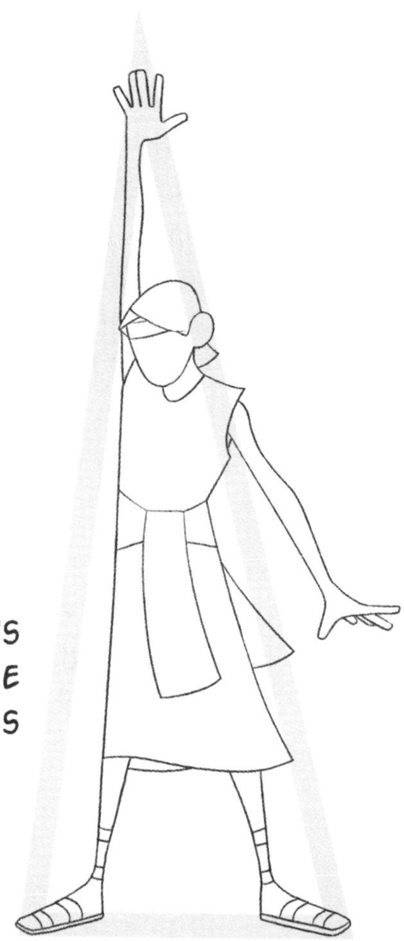

❸ DEFINE ALL THE FORMS. WHAT I LIKE ABOUT THIS POSE IS THE TRIANGLE THAT'S MADE. THE TRIANGLE IS THE STRONGEST SHAPE IN NATURE, SO USING IT IN A POSE GIVES THE FEELING OF STRENGTH AND SOLIDITY.

❹ DRAW THE DETAILS. REMEMBER WHICH KIND OF FOLDS GO WHERE TO BEST DESCRIBE THE FIGURE UNDERNEATH.

❺ BLOCK IN COLOR OR BLACK. AS WITH MOST OF THE CHARACTERS, I WENT WITH THE "STRIPED" LOOK OF DARK, LIGHT, DARK, LIGHT TO KEEP IT INTERESTING.

SARIAH

❶ BLOCK IN THE SHAPES. SINCE THE BABY IS SUCH A BIG PART OF THE COMPOSITION, WE'LL ADD IT IN NOW AND WORK AROUND IT.

❷ DRAW IN THE CLOTHES. IN THIS SITUATION, YOU WOULD MOST LIKELY SEE THE SLEEVE HANGING DOWN FROM HER BACK ARM. SINCE YOU CAN'T SEE THAT ARM, IT LOOKED FUNNY TO HAVE THE SLEEVE SO I DECIDED TO TAKE IT OUT. FEEL FREE TO ADD OR REMOVE WHATEVER YOU NEED TO MAKE THE DRAWING LOOK BETTER.

❸ DEFINE FORMS. THIS STEP IS PRETTY STRAIGHTFORWARD. AS WITH OTHER DRAWINGS, HER HEAD WOULDN'T SIT RIGHT IN LINE WITH HER SHOULDERS LIKE THAT, BUT I CHOSE TO DO IT TO KEEP A CONTINUOUS, FLOWING LINE.

4 DETAILS! JUST AS WITH HAIR, ANY FOLDS OR LINES IN THE CLOTHES (ESPECIALLY IN THE WRAP AROUND HER HEAD) SHOULD DESCRIBE THE DIRECTION AND FLOW. THERE IS A CLEAR SEPARATION BETWEEN THE NECK AND HEAD SECTIONS.

5 BLOCK IN COLOR OR BLACK. THE BLACK NOT ONLY MAKES THINGS MORE INTERESTING, BUT YOU CAN ALSO USE IT TO DRAW ATTENTION TO WHEREVER YOU WANT. IN THIS CASE SARIAH'S FACE AND THE BABY.

TEANCUM

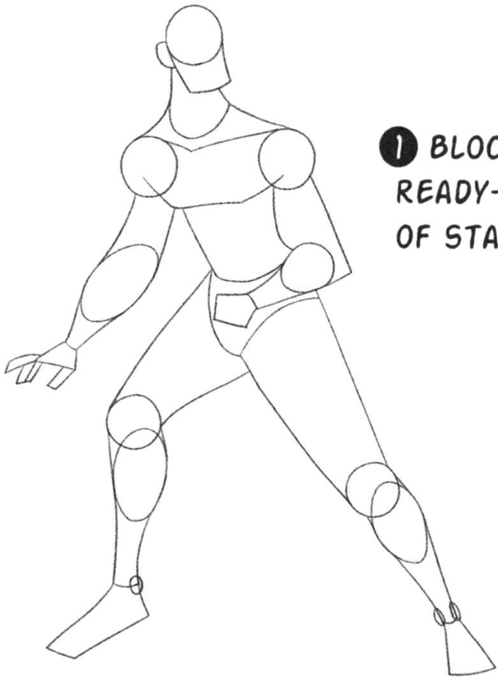

❶ BLOCK IN THE SHAPES. LET'S GIVE HIM A WIDE BASE AND A READY-FOR-ACTION POSE. THE WIDE BASE GIVES THE SENSE OF STABILITY AND STRENGTH.

❷ DRAW CLOTHES OVER THE FORM. PUTTING THE HEADBAND TAILS TO THE LEFT SHOW THAT HE WHIPPED HIS HEAD TO THE LEFT AND HEIGHTENS THE SENSE OF ACTION AND MOVEMENT.

❸ DEFINE THE FORMS.

4 DRAW IN ALL THE DETAILS.

5 FILL IN AREAS WITH BLACK OR COLOR.

LEARNING TO DRAW SHOULD INCLUDE MORE THAN JUST SKETCHING PEOPLE. LUCKILY, DRAWING PRINCIPLES DON'T CHANGE JUST BECAUSE YOUR SUBJECT DOES. AS YOU GO THROUGH, BE SURE TO START BY SIMPLIFYING THE FORM INTO SHAPES AND BUILDING FROM THERE.

MY HOPE IS THAT NOT ONLY WILL IT BE FUN TO DRAW SOMETHING DIFFERENT, BUT ALSO THAT BY DOING SO, YOU CAN SEE THAT NO MATTER WHAT YOU ARE DRAWING, IT CAN BE MADE EASIER BY FOLLOWING A FEW SIMPLE STEPS.

ONE THING THAT I DO WANT YOU TO TAKE NOTE OF IS **ANATOMY**: THE WAY ANIMAL BODIES ARE SHAPED. IF YOU LOOK AT THE BONE STRUCTURE OF MOST FOUR-LEGGED ANIMALS, THEY ARE SIMILAR TO HUMANS, JUST SQUASHED AND STRETCHED IN SOME PLACES. HOPEFULLY THE SIMILARITIES MAKE THINGS A BIT EASIER AS YOU GO THROUGH.

COW

❶ BLOCK IN THE SHAPES. IT DOESN'T MATTER WHETHER YOU ARE DRAWING A PERSON, AN ANIMAL, OR EVEN A **TREE—EVERYTHING** CAN BE BROKEN DOWN INTO BASIC SHAPES.

❷ DRAW IN THE FORMS AND DETAILS. SINCE WE ARE NOT DRAWING CLOTHES AND THE DRAWING IS PRETTY SIMPLE, WE CAN SPEED UP THE PROCESS A BIT.

❸ DARKEN OR COLOR IN AREAS.

ELEPHANT

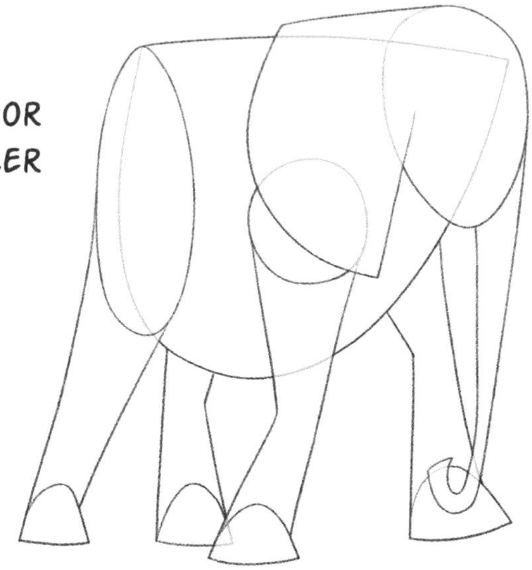

❶ BLOCK IN THE SHAPES. WHEN DEALING WITH ANIMAL OR HUMAN PROPORTIONS, A BIGGER HEAD AND SMALLER BODY SHOWS YOUTH.

❷ DRAW IN THE FORMS AND DETAILS. ELEPHANT NAILS ARE NOT ALL TOGETHER AS I DREW THEM ON THE FEET HERE. I MADE A DESIGN DECISION BECAUSE I JUST LIKE THE WAY IT LOOKS! ALWAYS FEEL FREE TO CHANGE ANYTHING IF YOU DON'T LIKE THE LOOK.

❸ DARKEN OR COLOR IN.

HORSE

❶ BLOCK IN THE SHAPES. WHEN BREAKING THINGS DOWN INTO SHAPES, IT DOESN'T ONLY HAVE TO BE CIRCLES, SQUARES, AND TRIANGLES. IF YOU LOOK AT THE HORSE, I USE A BEAN FOR THE BODY, LEAF SHAPES FOR EARS, AND A CURL FOR THE TAIL.

❷ DRAW IN THE FORMS AND DETAILS.

❸ DARKEN OR COLOR IN. THERE ARE A LOT OF DIFFERENT HORSES. YOU CAN DRAW AND COLOR SPOTS OR SPLOTCHES, OR YOU CAN HAVE THE WHOLE BODY BE LIGHT OR DARK. BE SURE TO PLAY WITH IT TO SEE WHAT YOU LIKE BEST.

GOAT

❶ BLOCK IN THE SHAPES.

❷ DRAW IN THE FORMS AND DETAILS. ONE OF THE MOST RECOGNIZABLE FEATURES ON A GOAT IS THE EYES. ASIDE FROM RECTANGULAR PUPILS, BE SURE TO ADD THE HAIR UNDER THE CHIN AND A FEW TUFTS OF FUR AROUND THE BODY.

❸ DARKEN OR COLOR IN.

LEOPARD

❶ BLOCK IN THE SHAPES.

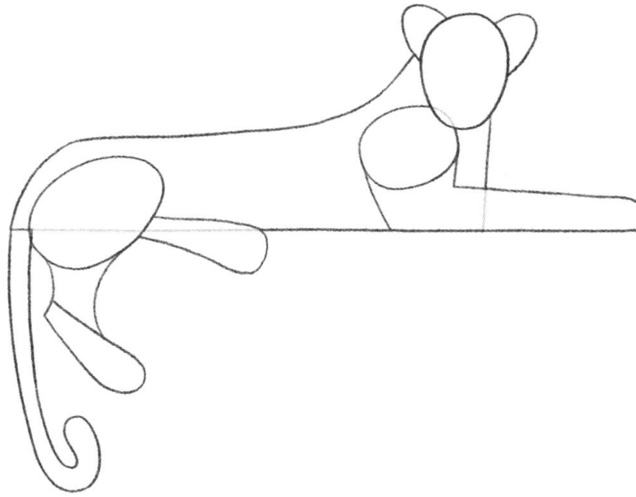

❷ DRAW IN THE FORMS AND DETAILS. THE SPOTS MAY SEEM LIKE A LOT TO DO, BUT TAKE IT A LITTLE BIT AT A TIME. HERE'S WHAT I DID:

EACH SPOT STARTS WITH A CIRCLE. (IT DOESN'T HAVE TO BE A CIRCLE. THAT'S JUST WHAT I CHOSE.)

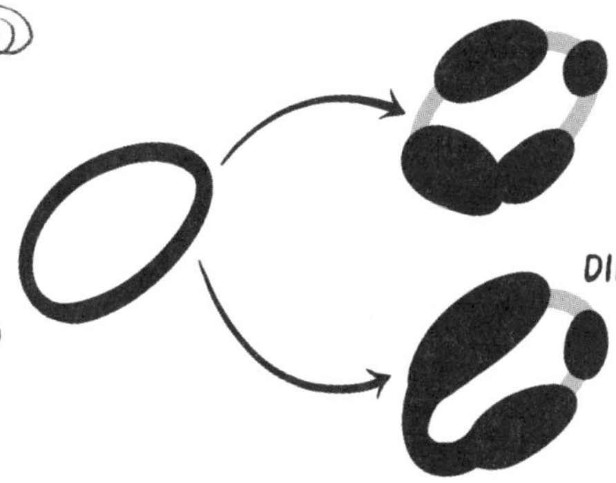

USING THE CIRCLE AS A GUIDE, DRAW DIFFERENT-SIZED DOTS

❸ DARKEN OR COLOR IN. EACH LEOPARD HAS DIFFERENT SPOTS AND DIFFERENT COLORING, SO FEEL FREE TO MAKE WHATEVER COLORS AND PATTERNS YOU WANT.

OWL

❶ BLOCK IN THE SHAPES. I KNOW THAT RIGHT NOW IT LOOKS LIKE A BAT WITH SQUARE WINGS, BUT THE MOST IMPORTANT THING IN THE FIRST STEP IS TO GET THE OVERALL SHAPE CORRECT.

❷ DRAW IN THE FORMS AND DETAILS. I OVERLAYED THE SHAPES FROM STEP 1 SO YOU CAN SEE JUST WHERE I BROKE THEM UP WITH THE FEATHERS.

❸ DARKEN OR COLOR IN. IF YOU LOOK AT A PICTURE OF A GREAT HORNED OWL, YOU WILL SEE ALL THE STRIPING IT HAS ON ITS FEATHERS. YOU CAN MAKE THIS STEP AS SIMPLE OR AS DETAILED AS YOU WANT.

PIG

❶ BLOCK IN THE SHAPES. A PIG'S LEGS AREN'T ACTUALLY THIS SHORT, BUT LIKE I SAID ON THE ELEPHANT DRAWING, THE BIGGER HEAD MAKES HIM LOOK YOUNGER AND CUTE. DRAWING HIS LEGS SHORT REALLY MAKES HIS HEAD FEEL LARGE.

❷ DRAW IN THE FORMS AND DETAILS. PIGS HAVE HAIR OVER THEIR WHOLE BODY, EVEN THOUGH THEY DO LOOK ALMOST SMOOTH. ONLY PUTTING A FEW TUFTS OF HAIR GIVES JUST THE RIGHT TEXTURE.

❸ DARKEN OR COLOR IN.

SHEEP

❶ BLOCK IN THE SHAPES. I PUT THE LEGS RIGHT NEXT TO EACH OTHER TO GIVE A FEELING OF MEEKNESS. WHENEVER YOU LAY OUT SHAPES, THE OVERALL FEEL YOU WANT THE CHARACTER TO HAVE SHOULD ALREADY BE CLEAR.

❷ DRAW IN THE FORMS AND DETAILS. TEXTURE IS A VERY IMPORTANT PART OF ANY DRAWING, BE IT AN ANIMAL, CLOTHING, OR A BUILDING. YOU CAN DRAW THE FLUFF ANY WAY YOU WANT; JUST BE SURE THAT IT LOOKS NICE AND SOFT!

❸ DARKEN OR COLOR IN.

SNAKE

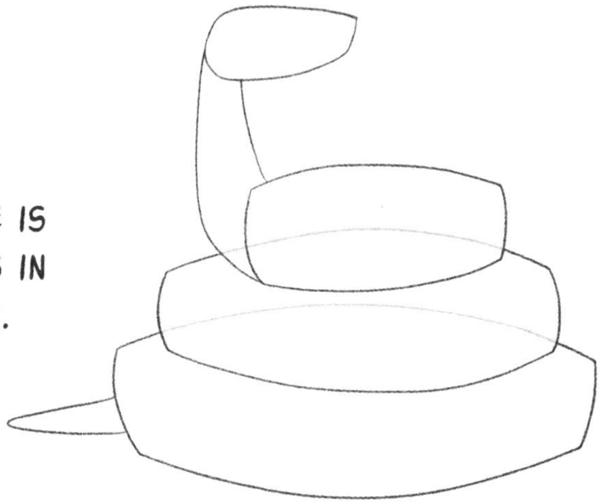

❶ BLOCK IN THE SHAPES. EVEN THOUGH THE SNAKE IS COILED, NOT JUST STACKED, JUST GET THE SHAPES IN FIRST AND WORRY ABOUT CONNECTING THEM LATER.

❷ DRAW IN THE FORMS AND DETAILS. AS I MENTIONED BEFORE, THE BIGGEST THING IN THIS STEP IS TO CONNECT THE COILS AROUND THE BACK OF THE FORM.

❸ DARKEN OR COLOR IN.

WWW.JEFFHARVEYART.COM